PRAISE FOR SEVEN MARKS OF A NEW TESTAMENT CHURCH

I believe it is fair to say that I know Brother David Black. He has been my professor, and I have been one of his pastors. On a trip to Ethiopia, I recall asking his wife (Becky), "What are Dr. Black's strengths?" She responded, "Seeing the big picture and making it simple for everyone to understand." *Seven Marks of a New Testament Church* is such a book. Clear, concise, engaging, and oozing with heavenly wisdom that will stir your heart and mind to want "gospel-maturity" for the glory of Christ.

Dr. Jason Evans
Pastor/Elder, Bethel Hill Baptist Church

Just when I thought I had read my favorite book by Dave Black, out comes this one! Whether God just saved you or you've been walking with Jesus for many years, this book is for you. Jesus says in Matt. 16:18, "I will build My church." From Jesus' perspective the church was future, it was his possession, and he was its architect! Today, we are tempted to forget about its inception, to view it as someone else's possession, and to build it with human minds and hands. Second to a wrong view of the gospel, nothing can hurt the Great Commission more than a wrong view of the church. Black's *Seven Marks of a New Testament Church* is a necessary reminder that we are to "do" church on God's terms, not our own. I, for one, have greatly benefited from Black's careful study of Acts 2:37–47. Believe me when I say, we can't afford to neglect these eleven verses if we hope to see God turn the world "upside down" in our day (Acts 17:6).

Dr. Thomas W. Hudgins
Capital Seminary and Graduate School

Well, Dave Black has done it again! In his book *Seven Marks of a New Testament Church* he brings to light the fact that much of what is being done in our twenty-first century churches bears little to no resemblance to what the Bible teaches. Ouch! But, it's true! Dave calls us to take a look at how we "do church" and seek to bring reform. It's not that we've chosen to be disobedient or unbiblical in an intentional way. Yet, much like ocean tides eat away a sand castle, biblical truths are being eroded by our man-made traditions and philosophies regarding church leadership, polity and fellowship. Anyone desiring to lead or be a part of what looks like a first century church should heartily welcome the simple, yet profound principles outlined by Dave from the book of Acts. Thanks again for challenging the status quo Brother Dave!

D. Kevin Brown
Pastor/Elder, Mt. Pleasant Baptist Church

Seven Marks

of A

New Testament Church

A Guide for Christians of All Ages

David Alan Black

Energion Publications
Gonzalez, FL
2014

Unless otherwise noted, Scripture translations are by the author.

Cover Design: Jody & Henry Neufeld
Cover Images:
Sunset, ID 3121126 © Koh Sze Kiat | Dreamstime.com
Cross, ID 35103100 © Maria Wachala | Dreamstime.com

ISBN10: 1-63199-046-2
ISBN13: 978-1-63199-046-5
Library of Congress Control Number: 2014943894

Energion Publications
P. O. Box 841
Gonzalez, FL 32560

energion.com
pubs@energion.com

TABLE OF CONTENTS

Acknowledgements iv
Introduction v

1   Evangelistic Preaching 1
2   Christian Baptism..9
3   Apostolic Teaching 17
4   Genuine Relationships...27
5   Christ-Centered Gatherings.....................................33
6   Fervent Prayer 39
7   Sacrificial Living..43

Acknowledgements

My thanks to Henry Neufeld (again!) for accepting this manuscript and for his constructive criticism and encouragement. Thanks also to my personal assistant, Jacob Cerone, for his extensive yet excellent work on this volume. I dedicate this book to my elders at Bethel Hill Baptist Church who weekly confirm the biblical principles set forth in this volume: Jason Evans, Jason Hatley, and Ed Johnson. But may the Head alone receive all the glory.

David Alan Black
Rosewood Farm, Virginia

Introduction

For years I have wanted to write a book on ecclesiology. This book, however, is not it. Instead, I have tried to ask the New Testament a very simple question: "What does a healthy, biblical church look like?" Of course, many excellent writers have attempted to answer this question. Books about the church are more abundant than ever. I do not claim to have found the only answer to this question. The one thing I have tried to do is allow the Scriptures to speak for themselves. You will notice that I asked my question *of the New Testament itself*, and it seems to me that the New Testament has provided us with an extraordinarily clear answer. The more I ponder the book of Acts, the more convinced I am that the wonderful chapter describing the birth of the church makes a fitting starting point for the study of New Testament ecclesiology. Should we ask, "Where do we start?", our course is already plotted, in eleven brief verses no less. I am speaking of Acts 2:37-47, verses that describe at least seven basic characteristics of the newly-formed church in Jerusalem. Hence the title: *Seven Marks of a New Testament Church*. Here is my translation of these verses:

> *Now when they heard this, they were cut to the heart and said to Peter and the other apostles, "Brothers, what should we do?" Peter said to them, "Repent, and be baptized every one of you in the name of Jesus Christ so that your sins may be forgiven, and you will receive the Holy Spirit as a gift. For the promise is for you, for your children, and for all who are far away, everyone whom the Lord our God calls to Him." And he testified with many other arguments and exhorted them, saying, "Be saved from this corrupt generation!" So those who welcomed his message were baptized, and that day about three thousand people were added to the group.*

They devoted themselves to the apostles' teaching, to the fellowship, to the breaking of the bread, and to the prayers. A deep sense of awe came over them all, and the apostles performed many miraculous signs and wonders. All the believers continued together in close fellowship and shared everything they had with one another. They would sell their property and possessions and distribute the money among all, according to what each person needed. Day after day they worshiped together in the temple and had meals together in their homes, eating with glad and humble hearts, all the while praising God and enjoying the goodwill of all the people. And every day the Lord kept adding to their group those who were being saved.

Before we examine this passage in greater detail, permit me to make four brief but important observations.

First, you will notice that I did not entitle my book *"The* Seven Marks of a New Testament Church." No human can claim such certainty. That would be to have omniscience. We may, of course, assert that we have discovered "the" marks of the church, but the definite article betrays not certainty but arrogance. In the second place, these seven descriptions of a New Testament church are valid regardless of one's denominational affiliation. After all, in the first century there were no Baptists or Presbyterians or Methodists or Catholics per se. These marks, I should think, would apply no less to modern mega-churches as to the joyous house churches of the first century. In the third place, it needs to be noted that the church in Acts 2 was hardly perfect. Remember, it was not the Jerusalem church that initiated the evangelism of Samaria or Antioch. That torch had to be passed to others. Even Peter did not yet fully understand the place the Gentiles would have in the church. Still, the church in Acts 2 exhibited all the vital signs of new life in Christ. A church can be exemplary and not be perfect. The key is that it must be moving in the right direction. Finally, we will study these marks in the order in which the text presents them to us. The reader will, no doubt, appreciate the logical and natural progression.

I am rather reluctant to add to the number of books on Acts. But I do want to awaken Christians to what these early followers of Jesus achieved. Their story is a remarkable one, and we would do well to emulate it. There is nothing new or profound in what I have written here. This is a simple book that any Christian can follow, even the newest believer. Quotations from the New Testament are my own translations made from the original Greek. In case you're wondering, the seven characteristics we'll be discussing are:

- Evangelistic preaching
- Christian baptism
- Apostolic teaching
- Genuine relationships
- Christ-centered gatherings
- Fervent prayer
- Sacrificial living

All over the globe there is a beautiful but powerful grassroots movement in the church asking the question, "What does a healthy congregation look like?" Many are looking for a simple, biblical definition of "church." Perhaps The First Church of Jerusalem can provide us with some answers. I hope so!

EVANGELISTIC PREACHING

"Peter said to them, 'Repent'."

In this book we are looking at the characteristics that marked the early church in Acts and how these characteristics might mark our churches today. It is clear, to start with, that a New Testament church is of necessity an evangelistic church. The first purpose of the church is to connect people to Jesus Christ. This is called the "Great Commission," and it is good news in every way. Here's how Matthew recorded it (Matt. 28:19-20):

> So wherever you go, train everyone you meet — the people in every nation — how to be My followers. Mark them publicly by baptism in the triune name of God: Father, Son, and Holy Spirit. Then instruct them not just in knowledge but in the practice of everything I've commanded you. And as you do this, remember: I will be with you, day after day after day, until the very end of the age.

Mark's version is as follows: "Go everywhere in the world and share the Good News with everyone" (Mark 16:15). Proclaiming the Good News of the Gospel was a decisive factor in the formation and growth of the early church. For it is here, in the event that happened at Calvary and on the first Easter Sunday, that the Christian church distinguishes itself from all the world's religions. See how carefully Luke expounds this theme in our text (Acts 2:37-41):

> Now when they heard this, they were cut to the heart and said to Peter and the other apostles, "Brothers, what should we do?" Peter said to them, "Repent, and be baptized every one of you in the name of Jesus Christ so that your sins may be forgiven, and you will receive the Holy Spirit as a gift. For the promise is for you, for your children, and for all who are far away, everyone whom

the Lord our God calls to Him." And he testified with many other
arguments and exhorted them, saying, "Be saved from this corrupt
generation!" So those who welcomed his message were baptized,
and that day about three thousand people were added to the group.

Clearly the risen Savior is eager to add new members to His body. So when we say that evangelistic preaching is the first mark of the church, what is meant is that a healthy church, like a healthy body, is always growing. Hence the first Christians were committed to evangelistic outreach. They were faithful to the duty their Master had placed on them. There was a whole world out there waiting to hear the Good News. Opportunities abounded for infusing the love of Christ into sin-sickened hearts. And the early Christians made the most of them. That is the sort of commitment that packs power in the twenty-first century, as it did in the first.

Of course, there is an entirely different way of looking at "preaching" today, and it would be helpful for us to consider it briefly. The trend in recent years is to apply the term "preaching" to the modern thirty-minute sermon delivered on Sunday mornings. It is the pastor, we are told, and not the evangelist, who is in view when the idea of preaching is under consideration. This understanding will not stand. In the first place, it is plain from the New Testament that preaching takes place in an evangelistic context. The sermons in Acts are good examples of this. Note that the lost, not the saved, were the objects of Peter's preaching on the Day of Pentecost. And so it is elsewhere in Acts. In the second place, to call New Testament pastors "preachers" is to ignore the biblical texts that consistently portray the role of pastor as that of teacher. Two texts are of greatest importance here: Eph. 4:11 ("And He gifted some to be apostles, some prophets, some evangelists, and some *pastor-teachers*....") and 1 Tim. 3:2 ("Now an overseer must be above reproach, the husband of one wife, temperate, sensible, respectable, hospitable, *able to teach*...."). If, therefore, we would retain the New Testament's own perspective on the role of a pastor, we must be wary of applying the term "preaching" to what takes place when believers gather for mutual edification. Preaching is neither the sole nor primary task of pastor-teachers. It is simply sharing the Good News, and the first believers were so successful at it that they were accused of "turning the world upside down" (Acts 17:6). The Christians of New Testament days saw bold evangelism as the purpose for which the church existed.

But what exactly *is* evangelism? And how is it to be practiced today? There are at least five characteristics that always mark genuine evangelism. Let us examine them a little more closely.

A *Christ-exalting message* is perhaps the first characteristic that strikes us. Evangelism is neither a system nor a method. It is simply bringing people face to face with a Person. It is sharing the Good News of what God has done in Jesus Christ through His death and resurrection. It is the wonderful story of how God rescues people in their need and transforms them into a new society. And note: There is nothing shallow about this message. The Gospel is a life-changing message, and the Christians who first turned the world upside down knew it.

Do we truly understand this message, and are we able to share it with others? We would be wise to store away in our memories certain key verses from Scripture that summarize the Gospel. A good example is 1 Cor. 15:1-4. Here we see that Paul had a deep assurance of the truth of what he was preaching, and supremely of the reality of the death, burial, resurrection, and post-resurrection appearances of Christ. Conversion is unthinkable without such an understanding of the significance of Calvary and the empty tomb. Another passage is Rom. 10:9-10. Unless we confess Jesus as Lord and believe that God raised Him from the dead, we cannot be saved. The intellectual content of saving faith can be as simple as "Jesus is Lord" (1 Cor. 12:2). This confession, indeed, lies at the heart of every true conversion.

We must, then, immerse ourselves in the Word we proclaim. This is an age of relativity, but people are crying out for truth. It is up to us to explain the Gospel to them in words they can grasp. Like the early Christians, we must discover the need for a Jesus-centered presentation, however flexible our evangelistic methods might be. This means that, like the apostles in Acts, we must always seek to exalt Christ in our preaching. The early Christians were consumed with a passion for Jesus. No one else was so important to them. If people have really found the Good News, they will always be eager to tell others of Jesus and His love. And there is nothing so attractive in this world as a church in which Jesus is exalted.

A second characteristic that stands out when we think of evangelism is its *Spirit-dependence.* As David Wells puts it in his book *God the Evangelist,* it is the Holy Spirit who initiates, motivates, and empowers evangelism. Indeed, the Holy Spirit is the supreme actor in the book of Acts, and He was the source of power in the lives of the earliest disciples. It was the Spirit who launched the first evangelistic outreach on the Day of Pentecost (Acts 2:38 ff.), and it was the Spirit who stirred up the hearts of the believers in Antioch to begin evangelizing Asia Minor (Acts 13-14). The same theme is apparent throughout Acts. These followers of Jesus lived in total dependence on the Holy Spirit. Nothing was allowed to hinder His power in their lives.

What about us? We know little of the Spirit's presence and power today. We rely instead on our methods, education, and finances. Perhaps there is no greater challenge to the contemporary church than to repent of our overdependence on manmade evangelistic strategies. The first Christians sought to be filled with the Spirit (Eph. 5:18) and to obey Him (Acts 5:32). Soul-winning was just that simple for them. They knew that evangelism was impossible without staying in close communion with their unseen Guide. If we wish to see a resurgence of the evangelistic fervor that marked the early church, we must have the same commitment. A. W. Tozer, the famous Bible teacher, is very explicit about the Spirit's role in evangelism (*Paths of Power,* p.9):

> The church began in power, moved in power, and moved just as long as she had power. When she no longer had power, she dug in for safety. But her blessings were like manna. When they tried to keep it overnight, it bred worms and stank. So we have had monasticism, scholasticism, institutionalism — all indicative of one thing: absence of spiritual power. In church history every return

to the New Testament has been marked by a new advance somewhere, a fresh proclamation of the gospel and an upsurge of missionary zeal.

We need to take this warning seriously. Just as the Holy Spirit commissioned Jesus for servanthood and empowered Him for witness, so He desires to do the same thing in our lives today. The book of Acts shows what God can do through men and women who are empowered by the Spirit. If you allow Him, the Spirit will come and bear witness to Christ through you. This is the promise of our Lord (Acts 1:8).

A third characteristic of evangelism that was highly evident among the first Christians is its *equal-opportunity nature.* It was not a task that was delegated to the leadership alone. All were to share the Good News with their neighbors. Thus Jude can urge his readers to "save some by snatching them out of the fire" (Jude 23), while Paul can commend the newly fledged Thessalonian believers for "trumpeting forth the Word of God" (1 Thess. 1:8). Every believer was expected to do the work of evangelism wherever they went. Now if every Christian is called to be a witness, and if every church has a global mission at its doorstep, why are only certain people called "missionaries," and why do boards and agencies try to do the work of the local church? There is not a single hint in the New Testament that the early Christians saw evangelism as the responsibility of certain professionals. Of course, people and agencies that work with and through the local church may be said to be fulfilling their mission responsibility. But in reality, every one of us ought to be a "full-time missionary."

We could take all this much further. I have tried to do so in my book *Will You Join the Cause of Global Missions?* Jesus Himself was the ultimate missionary, and He entrusted to His followers world missions. Even if we cannot travel to a foreign field, the "uttermost parts of the world" have come to us. Just look at any college or university campus today. Missiologists call this "global missions in reverse," but it is no less missions. That's why I was so pleased to hear that one of my doctoral students in New Testament was recently asked to teach communications at a secular university. I imagine he will do more than disseminate information, too. I can see him giving himself in time-consuming acts of missional love simply because they are needed. After all, sharing one's faith is simply helping another person take a step closer to Jesus. If you want evangelism in your church, do not call for a professional evangelist. Equip your people for Gospel witness. The results will amaze you.

In the fourth place, evangelism in the New Testament was always characterized by *genuine concern for the social needs of the lost*. When I was in seminary, a good deal of distrust existed between those who emphasized personal salvation in evangelism and those who emphasized the so-called social gospel. The two, however, are indivisible. Writes John Stott in his outstanding book *Balanced Christianity* (p. 46):

> It is true that the risen Lord Jesus left his church a Great Commission to preach, to evangelise, and to make disciples. And this commission is still binding upon the church. But the commission does not supersede the commandment, as if 'you shall love your neighbour' were now replaced by 'you shall preach the gospel'. Nor does it re-interpret neighbor-love in exclusively evangelistic terms. Instead, it enriches the commandment to love our neighbor by adding to it a new and Christian dimension, namely the duty to make Christ known to him.

It is worth reflecting for a moment on what Stott is saying. For example, what led the pagan community in Antioch to coin the term "Christians" to describe the followers of the Way in their midst (Acts 11:26)? Was it not their new "Way" of life, their Christ-like behavior? These "Christians" were nothing other than the hands and feet of Jesus in their world. They proclaimed *and* cared. And so it should be with us today. We separate evangelism and social care to our own injury. No one can be a genuine Christian without letting Christ serve others through him or her. Of course, proclamation of the Gospel is primary. Yet proclamation without presence is a failure, and the first Christians were certainly not guilty of it.

Our churches have to get back to this balance if there is to be successful evangelism in our day. Nothing authenticates the Gospel like a passionate concern for people's needs and an involvement in their daily struggles. I think of the health center my wife and I established in Ethiopia several years ago. People came for healing, and many of them left born again. There was no need to convince the patients of their physical predicament. They were well aware of that! They needed to understand that Jesus cared about their *whole* person — body, soul, and spirit. Many have found Jesus' own example helpful in this regard. A classic text is Matt. 9:35: "Then Jesus went about all the cities and villages, teaching in their synagogues, proclaiming the good news of the kingdom, and healing every disease and every sickness." Not only did Jesus teach and preach — He healed! Not only did He feed the multitudes — He told them where the Bread of Life could be found! Social compassion, then, is not an optional extra for those who like that sort of thing. It is absolutely essential. We are not to overvalue social involvement, but neither are we to despise it. In short, if you believe Jesus Christ, you can scarcely ignore the social needs of people.

There is a final characteristic of evangelism in the early church that we would be foolish to neglect, and that is its *emphasis on follow-up*. It would be impossible to exaggerate the importance of after-care in the life of the early church. The earliest Christians were not content with the hit-and-run tactics of some modern-day evangelists. Notice how follow-up is described in Acts 2:41-42:

> *So those who welcomed his message were baptized, and that day about three thousand people were added to the group. They devoted themselves to the apostles' teaching and to the fellowship, to the breaking of the bread and to the prayers.*

New believers need teaching and fellowship, and the early church took great pains to see that these needs were met. That has a lot to say to the modern church. I cannot help being struck by the way we undervalue after-care. It amazes me that some can claim "twenty professions of faith" and not give testimony of how these new converts are being nurtured. It is interesting to observe that baptism seems to have been administered immediately after one's profession of faith. We shall see in our next chapter how important that act of obedience is. Suffice it to say here that in our eagerness to make "decisions" for Christ, we all too often fail to make "disciples" as we are commanded to do (Matt. 28:19-20). Unless there is careful follow-up, very little is likely to become of the profession.

In subsequent chapters we shall look in detail at this matter of after-care. But there is one final point I wish to make in this chapter. As we have seen, there is a tremendous amount of evangelism taking place in the book of Acts. This is not surprising in light of Jesus' words, "You shall be My witnesses" (Acts 1:8). In Acts, witnessing is central. It is a sign of genuine spiritual life, and it is to be our top priority. It is not good enough to claim "I am a follower of Jesus." If we are followers of Jesus, then we are to become His witnesses. And why can we not do that? If we do not make evangelism a matter of the greatest importance as the earliest Christians did, we will reap the consequences for our neglect. Evangelism is the supreme instrument of church growth. That's why the early church made it such a high priority, and that is why our churches must do the same. If we are to profit from the example of these early Christians, there are few areas to which we need to pay closer attention than to the way they joyfully and passionately shared the Good News with others. Once we grasp their joy and passion, it will be impossible for us to sit back and rest on our laurels.

2 CHRISTIAN BAPTISM

"Then those who had welcomed his message were baptized, and that day about 3,000 people were added to their number."

The second notable mark impossible to doubt in the life of the early church is the importance the first believers attached to Christian baptism. It is hard for us today to realize the life-changing significance of that event from our perspective 2,000 years later. We hardly have any idea what it meant to take such a radical step of obedience. Baptism today is often merely a ceremony to be tacked on to our conversion, sometimes months or even years after we come to faith. I have even heard of people postponing their baptism until they could travel to Israel in order to be "baptized where Jesus was baptized." Perhaps Philip should have ordered the eunuch's chariot to make a U-turn so that his Ethiopian convert could be baptized in the Jordan!

So many Christians miss it at this point. But the early church had no doubts about the importance of baptism. Much could be said about the practice of baptism in the early church, but six features in particular seem to emerge from a reading of the book of Acts.

The first one is the *immediacy* of baptism. What I mean is this. In the book of Acts you will sometimes find conversion accompanied by the gift of speaking in tongues. But at every stage in the advance of the early church, new converts were baptized. It was part and parcel of their salvation experience. You got saved, and you got wet (see Acts 2:41; 8:12-13, 36-38; 9:18; 10:44-48; 16:15, 33; 18:8; 19:4-5; 22:15). It is an undeniable fact that the earliest Christians thought that baptism was a vital part of the Christian life, so much so that baptism was administered as soon as possible after a person had come to faith in Christ. Lack of instruction did not stop them.

The reason it did not stop them is bound up, in the second place, with the *significance* of baptism. Paul makes it clear in Rom. 6:1-4 what baptism means. Baptism is a wonderful portrayal of the Christian's initial identification with Christ. It pictures the believer's dying and rising again with Christ "to walk in newness of life" (6:4). It is the "Messiah's badge," if you will, of the new people of God. Baptism, moreover, is a sign of the Spirit's work. At conversion, believers experience the baptism of the Holy Spirit. "By one Spirit we were all baptized into one body," is the way Paul describes it in 1 Cor. 12:13. Water baptism is a symbol of the reception of the Holy Spirit into our lives and of our identification with Christ's body, the local church. Spirit and water baptism thus belong together. They are two sides of the same coin. Hence Paul can write to the Ephesian believers, "There is one Lord, one faith, and one baptism" (Eph. 4:6). "But Paul," you ask, "to which baptism are you referring — Spirit or water?" Such a question would scarcely have been asked by the earliest Christians, among whom baptism (as we have said) was administered as soon as possible after profession of faith. The expression "unbaptized believer" would have been an oxymoron to them! Spirit baptism obviously came first, but it was followed, as soon as possible, by water baptism.

I believe that churches today would do well to follow this pattern. I realize that the pattern *baptism-then-instruction* is counter-intuitive. Many churches, including some in the Majority World, think it best to delay baptism until after a time of intense teaching. After all, it is reasoned, how can we judge the genuineness of a person's profession without a period of initiation and testing? Humanly speaking, I do not disagree in the least with this way of thinking. To me it is both logical and practical. But the real question is: What does Scripture say? That is the question we must always ask. And what is the *scriptural* answer? There are at least two biblical reasons why Christian baptism should follow conversion immediately. The first is the command of our Lord Himself. In Matt. 28:19-20, Jesus gave us clear instructions. Note the order:

baptizing, *and then teaching.* This order is not optional; we have no right to reverse it! But there is a second reason why we should insist on immediate baptism, and that is the pattern set forth for us by the early church. When we look at the actual way the early Christians sought to fulfill the Great Commission, we see a remarkable contrast with the way we do things in the modern church. In accordance with the command of their Lord, the early church did not interpose a period of catechism between conversion and baptism. Both the Ethiopian eunuch (Acts 8) and the Philippian jailor (Acts 16) are good examples of this. We should, accordingly, be wary of altering our practices to suit our own logic. Indeed, "What God has joined together, let not man put asunder." The example of the early church calls us to repent, and then to implement the pattern of immediate baptism with renewed seriousness.

The third feature of Christian baptism is its *distinction from Jewish baptism.* Baptism for New Testament believers was very different from the Jewish washings with which the earliest Christians, being Jews, were familiar. Two things in particular set Christian baptism apart from Jewish baptism. In the first place, Christian baptism was never self-administered. It was always performed by another. What a marvelous picture of our salvation! The agent in our salvation is Christ; we are merely recipients. Moreover, we can contribute nothing to our salvation; it is a gift of grace that cannot be earned but only received.

The second way in which Christian baptism is distinguished from Jewish baptism is the fact that it was unrepeatable. It is a once-for-all event. Jewish baptisms took place frequently. This was not the case with Christian baptism. So important was this distinction that the author of Hebrews considers it to be one of the six foundational truths of Christianity (see Heb. 6:2). Here "instruction about washings" refers to the difference between Christian baptism and similar Jewish rites such as proselyte baptism, John's baptism, and the baptisms of the Qumran sect. Scripturally speaking, there is only one baptism for Christians, and it does not have to be repeated.

Fourthly, in reading the book of Acts one is struck by the *public nature* of Christian baptism. On the Day of Pentecost, for example, we read that some 3,000 believers were baptized. Archeology suggests that these new converts availed themselves of the many baptismal pools (*mikvot*) located near the entrance to the temple mount, a very public place indeed. Friends and relatives of those being baptized undoubtedly witnessed this step of obedience. Clearly these Christians were not ashamed to make their new-found faith public. And their example is a poignant reminder for us today that baptism should be an observable act whenever possible. It is, one might say, the Christian's "pledge of allegiance" to Jesus Christ. To use a slightly different (though related) analogy: baptism is the wedding ring we place on our finger during our marriage ceremony. The ring on our finger does not *make* us married. It is merely a symbol, and a beautiful one at that, that we *are* married. And be it observed: we do not wait a week or a month or a year after the wedding ceremony to begin wearing our ring. On the contrary, we are eager to let the whole world know that we are no longer single.

Baptism is like that wedding ring. It is a mark, impressed upon our physical bodies, that tells the whole world that we are no longer alone: we belong to Another, and we also belong to the people He calls His body. My own baptism in Hawaii was a very public event: it took place at Kailua Beach where I swam and surfed daily! I shall never forget my dismay when, several years later, our church decided to build an indoor baptistery. "It is more convenient than going to the beach," I was told. More convenient, yes, but more scriptural? Why should we move our baptisms indoors and abandon a golden opportunity to portray the Gospel to our unsaved neighbors and friends? I have yet to get a satisfactory answer to that question.

A fifth observation about Christian baptism is perhaps not so obvious but is implied in what we read in the book of Acts. And that is its *egalitarian nature*. By that I mean that anybody who had been born again could receive it, and anybody who had been born again could administer it. Baptism was for Jew and for Hellenist, for rich and for poor, for young and for old, for male and for female. Today we might say that Christian baptism is for conservative and for liberal, for Republican and for Democrat, for Whites and for Hispanics, for home-educated believers and for government-school-educated believers. Baptism, like the Lord's Supper (see chapter 5), is the great equalizer for the Christian. We *all* pass through the waters of baptism, and we are *all* obligated (and, I might add, enabled) to walk in newness of life. The decision to be baptized was, of course, an individual one, but salvation meant integration into a community of "those who were being saved" (Acts 2:47).

And who administered baptism? There is no evidence from Acts or from the New Testament epistles that this responsibility rested solely on the shoulders of the apostles or "ordained leadership." This should not surprise us. The essence of all New Testament teaching about church leadership is that leaders are to be enablers. They are not to do the work of the ministry as much as they are to prepare others to do that work (see Eph. 4:11-12). They are like NASCAR pit crews who will pump gas for you so that you can drive in the race. Although I have never been ordained, I had the privilege of baptizing my own children. Perhaps you have had a similar experience. Some may object, "But surely baptism ought to be administered by properly ordained ministers!" My answer is that I can find no evidence for this conclusion in Scripture. Christian "ministers" are no more priests, and no less, than any other member of Christ's body. When it is suggested that only ordained clergy can baptize new believers, this is something that is quite alien to the New Testament, which sees all believers as priests of the Most High God. Indeed, the Great Commission — going, baptizing, and teaching — belongs to every Christian, not to any ministerial group. Are we, then, to limit the ministry of baptism to ordained clergy? We may do so if we wish, but we shall find no warrant in the New Testament for our position. As Eduard Schweitzer notes in his book *Church Order in the New Testament* (p. 186), "The apostles do not as a rule baptise (Acts 10:48, cf. 19:5 beside 6a, 1 Cor. 1:14-17). Ordinary church members do (Acts 9:18)." Schweitzer's words are wisdom for today. We would do well to heed them.

It is instructive to note, in the sixth and final place, that Christian baptism required *courage*. It really put the earliest Christians on the spot! Little wonder that baptism is the climax of all the evangelistic sermons in Acts. Baptism is the way the early church clinched the commitment — not by the raising of a hand or the walking of an aisle or the signing of a pledge card. The act was simple but profound. "I have decided to follow Jesus," is the way the old song puts it. "I'm burning my bridges. There's no turning back." Saying that, and saying that publicly, will take boatloads of courage. But thank God: He "has not given us a spirit of fear, but of power, love, and a sound mind" (2 Tim. 1:7)!

Here are six things the earliest believers valued for their life and ministry. We have much to learn from them today. Baptism is a wonderful picture of our union with Christ. It is, as it were, the "price of admission" into the church. It is the first act of Christian obedience, the symbol that we have put off the old life and have been raised up to walk in newness of life. There is ample evidence that the early church considered baptism as the means of initiation into the church. The 3,000 converts on the Day of Pentecost were thus formed into a distinct community — an apostolic fellowship based on apostolic teaching. If we are to learn anything from these early Christians, we must discover anew the significance and blessing of Christian baptism. Have you received it yet, in total unworthiness and adoring gratitude?

It would not be proper to conclude this chapter without drawing attention to two areas of disagreement concerning Christian baptism that exists among committed followers of Jesus. The first question concerns the proper recipients of Christian baptism: should infants be baptized as well as adults? The second question has to do with the proper mode of baptism: is immersion the only scriptural mode of baptizing a person, or is sprinkling also allowed? My own conviction is that scriptural baptism is for believers only, by immersion only. But how did I come up with that conviction? And how should you arrive at yours?

There are three reasons why I hold to my position about baptism: upbringing and background, training, and personal Bible study. I have always been a Baptist. I was converted in a Baptist church, and I have attended Baptist churches ever since. That is my upbringing and background, neither of which, of course, guarantees that my beliefs are correct.

In the second place, there is my training. My education has reinforced my personal beliefs about baptism. Both Biola University and Talbot School of Theology (where I received my B.A. and M.Div. degrees, respectively) were Baptist-friendly institutions of higher education. Even when I went on to the University of Basel in Switzerland for my D.Theol. degree, I still encountered Baptist theology. I will never forget sitting in Markus Barth's lectures on the Gospel of Mark and hearing him defend believer's baptism, not once but several times, and at considerable length. And this in a Reformed university! Markus Barth was hardly alone in his views. His famous father, Karl Barth, had long objected to paedobaptism (the baptizing of infants) and even published a book on the subject (*The Teaching of the Church Regarding Baptism*).

Finally, there is the matter of my own personal study of Scripture. What guidance can Acts offer? I argue that the book of Acts does not specifically refer to the baptism of infants. "Household baptisms" indeed took place on at least five occasions, but one cannot prove, just from Scripture, that these households included infants or young children incapable of faith and repentance. Whenever the book of Acts speaks of baptism, it is never baptism without faith and repentance. Infant baptism simply makes no sense if you believe that an informed decision is necessary to be saved.

What should your position be on these controversial issues? It seems to me that your view will be shaped by the same three factors that shaped mine: your upbringing and background, your training, and (most important of all) your personal study of Scripture. A good deal has been written on the subject, and it must be confessed that a good deal of it rests more on assumptions than on the wrestling with the text of Scripture. As we mature in the Christian life, doctrine sometimes becomes more confusing, not less. We would be wise not to make our decision without serious prayer and Bible study. And even if we must agree to disagree with our Christian brethren on these matters, this is still no reason for the dismembering of the body of Christ. When Paul and Barnabas fell out with each other (the Greek of Acts 15:39 implies a "sharp disagreement"), they still continued their respective missionary work. And so must we whenever we face in-house disagreements. I am so grateful for the example of Bo Reicke, my "Doctor Father" in Basel, who nurtured me as a young scholar. This amazing man was a committed Lutheran and yet he could work with a committed Baptist. He had not only a scholar's mind but a pastor's heart, and today I am glad to be able to pay him the honor he is due. Unity does not demand uniformity. But it does imply interdependence. If the church fails to exhibit it, it contradicts the very Gospel of reconciliation it preaches.

3 APOSTOLIC TEACHING

"They devoted themselves to the apostles' teaching."

We now come to the third mark of a New Testament church, and that is its commitment to biblical truth. One of the weakest aspects of Western Christianity is our failure to give proper teaching to new converts. As a result, biblical illiteracy plagues the church in America. This is a weakness in some mainline churches, and often in evangelical churches too.

I recall once sitting on an examination committee for a Ph.D. student in New Testament. He had mastered a good deal of factual information about the New Testament — the major solutions to the synoptic problem, the various schools of textual criticism, the background to the Corinthian correspondence, and so forth — but he utterly failed to provide references when I quoted to him ten well-known verses from the New Testament. When he pleaded time constraints, I gently showed him why it is not enough to know *about* the New Testament; graduates in New Testament may well be expected to have a mastery of the New Testament itself. It is ironic that evangelical Christians, who often are loudest in their condemnation of biblical illiteracy, are often guilty of it themselves. Learning basic Christian doctrine is a vital part of discipleship. It begins with knowing certain facts about the Bible, but it also involves obeying the truths of Scripture. What we are after is a growing knowledge of the Lord Jesus Christ that will change our whole lives.

As we see from our text, the nurture of recent converts to Christianity is an area to which the earliest Christians gave tremendous care. The early church *prioritized* the word. We see this priority in Jerusalem when the apostles insisted that they should

give themselves "to the ministry of the word and prayer" (Acts 6:4).
We see it in Pisidian Antioch when the whole church gathered "to
hear the word of the Lord" (Acts 13:44). We see it in Ephesus when
people from all over Asia came and "heard the word of the Lord"
as Paul engaged in teaching for two years (Acts 19:10). Indeed, as
the word "grew," so did the church (Acts 6:7). This is a very remarkable thing. Early Christianity was unstoppable because it was
biblical to the core. And it all sprung from the original teaching
of the apostles.

Granted that the early church had a commitment to the
Scriptures, to know them and obey them, how were the Scriptures
taught? And who were the teachers? We can say three things.

1. The truth about Jesus Christ was originally taught by the
apostles themselves — men who had been with Jesus and who
had heard Him personally. It is clear from their use of the Old
Testament in their Gospel preaching that they were steeped in
the Scriptures. The Bible was fundamental to their way of living.
It was the milk that nurtured them (1 Pet. 2:2) and the meat that
enabled them to mature (Heb. 5:12-14). Eventually the apostles
(and their assistants) produced literature of their own — Gospels
and epistles and even a magnificent prophecy of the last days (the
book of Revelation). These early believers had no seminaries or
training centers or Bible conferences but they had truth. For them,
the word of God was "alive and powerful and sharper than any
two-edged sword" (Heb. 4:12).

That is still true today. Do you know of a church where there
is a love for the word of God? That will be a church where the
leaders study the Bible diligently and rely on it for guidance. Such a
church is also very likely to be a growing church, at least growing in
obedience. Recently the congregation in my home church decided
it was biblical to have elders. Previously, our leadership had taught
through the book of Acts, and a clear pattern of eldership emerged.
Eventually the congregation fairly cried out, "Why shouldn't we
have elders too?" But even more impressive was the love we so
clearly had for each other. The matter was fully discussed and the
decision deferred until we had come to a common mind. When as

congregations we study His word (and not just books about His word), we may expect to see the Holy Spirit lead us into truth and obedience. If only it would happen more often!

2. Another thing we learn from reading the New Testament is how varied the teaching ministry of the early church was. Nowadays we almost always focus on the ministry of the pulpit. "I go to Dr. So-and-So's church" — the good doctor usually being noted for his prowess in the pulpit. In a church like Corinth or Philippi, we might expect to find a "senior pastor" who was known for his "dynamic expository preaching." But you will find nothing of the sort in the pages of the New Testament. We do not even know the names of the pastors of the churches in the New Testament. (Timothy and Titus are often incorrectly referred to as "pastors.") The reason is clear. Leadership in the early church was a *shared* ministry. Their churches enjoyed a "fellowship of leadership" (the term is Michael Green's). How wise they were! There was no pulpit-centricity in these early congregations such as we find today in so many of our churches. Formal teaching undoubtedly existed. But this does not mean that the leaders did all the talking. Even Paul, when meeting with the believers in Troas, engaged in a dialogue with his audience rather than delivering a lengthy monologue (Acts 20:7).

Not only that. The Holy Spirit could lead several speakers to bring a word (1 Cor. 14:29), and believers themselves were expected to be "teaching and admonishing one another" (Col. 3:16). I believe there is no single lesson we need to learn more earnestly today than the importance of mutual ministry when it comes to the teaching of Scripture. To say this is not to belittle the ministry of pastor-teachers. I have trained a good number of them through the years! And who among us has never benefited from a message that was prayerful, biblical, Christ-exalting, and delivered in the power of the Spirit and with humility? Nor am I pleading for an "anything goes" mentality when it comes to our gatherings as believers. I am simply pleading for such a sensitivity to the Holy Spirit that it should not be impossible for the Spirit to get a message across to the people through *any* member of the congregation He should inspire to speak. This is no pipe dream on my part. I have seen it happen in many congregations, my own included. I believe that most churches could do a great deal more to encourage this outlook. In this way many in the congregation will be prepared to put into practice the teaching of Heb. 10:24-25. The gathering would move from being a time of passive listening to an opportunity to engage in mutual edification. There is nothing so attractive in the world as a gathering where Jesus is dominant, not one particular teacher, regardless of how able he may be. This was perhaps the supreme secret of the early church: it insisted that Jesus Christ Himself, the church's "Senior Pastor" (1 Pet. 5:4), have the first place *in everything* (Col. 1:18).

3. But what of personal Bible study? Let me call your attention to a wonderful verse, 1 John 2:27a: "But the anointing that you have received from the Holy Spirit remains in you, and you do not need for anyone to teach you." Did you see that? What John is saying is that when it comes to studying the Scriptures, the ball is ultimately in your court. It all boils down to this: If the Holy Spirit has come into your life, then you have everything you need to engage in serious Bible study. So has He? I suggest that before you go any further in this book you get this sorted out. It doesn't matter if you go to church or have your name written on a membership roll. It's a matter of being genuinely "born again" (John 3:3).

You see, when a person comes to Christ, a brand new life begins. Having found Christ, we desire above everything else to get to know Him more and more. This is the very essence of the Christian life. As Paul says, "My goal is to know Him" (Phil. 3:10). Do you have a genuine desire to know Christ? Are you hungry and thirsty for Him? What I want to ask Christians who have no desire to read the Bible is this: Do you really know the Lord? Love for Christ is a mark of being a Christian. Bible study is therefore very much a mark of discipleship, for how can we love a person and not want to know who that person is?

And so I ask: Do you know Christ? If you are in doubt, I want to point you to a New Testament letter that was written especially for you. We have already quoted from it. John wrote his First Letter so that his readers would know that they have eternal life. And in this short letter you will find several tests by which this new life will make itself transparent. The apostle John makes it crystal clear that when we come to know Jesus Christ personally, we begin a life of friendship with Him — a *personal* rather than *mediated* relationship that is meant to grow richer and richer until the day we meet Him "face to face" (1 John 3:1). John is emphasizing the sufficiency of the Holy Spirit when it comes to knowing spiritual truth. It is He who grants us understanding of the Scripture. It is He who allows us to grow in knowledge and in spiritual stature. It is He who illuminates to our hearts and minds not only the person of Christ but His will for our lives. The Spirit is thus the supreme interpreter of God's word. Once you understand this, Bible study will become an important part of your life, a discipline that you can hardly afford to neglect. This means that once we come to faith in Christ, we need never be dependent on human teachers to lead us, helpful though they may be. As our "anointing," the Holy Spirit not only teaches us the truth of God but guides us as we seek to live out that truth in our lives. We have in the Spirit a teacher who is resident within us to show us the mind of the Lord. Little wonder that increasing numbers of Christians today are finding that they have a new love for the Bible.

If God gives you that love, thank Him, and use it believingly, knowing that this is how the Spirit worked in the early church. I am not talking about making a fetish out of the Bible. We dare not fall into the trap of legalism when it comes to God's word. I have no advice for you as to when you should read the Bible, or how often. I have no desire to argue with you about which translation of the Bible is the "best" one. (The fact is that there are plenty of excellent Bible translations available today.) The important thing is that you meet with the Lord. Don't be afraid of variety. Your relationship with the Lord is just that: a relationship that cannot be reduced to a set of rules. Always remember that it is the Holy Spirit who allows you to understand what you are reading. Just as importantly, it is the Spirit who enables you to share life with your Friend. No, there is nothing wrong with a disciplined system of

Bible study. But there is everything wrong with worshipping your system or imposing it on others.

So then, our teachers are multifold: gifted leaders, our fellow Christians, and ultimately the Holy Spirit Himself. Are there any other implications of our brief look at teaching in the New Testament? Several things stand out.

In the first place, I am struck by the seriousness with which these early Christians took their responsibility to help each other grow in their faith. Mutual edification is absolutely necessary for Christian maturity. Indeed, we have much to learn from each other. Note that the very one who said "You do not need for anyone to teach you" was a teacher! It is an interesting and significant fact that the readers of Hebrews were exhorted to become "teachers" (Heb. 5:12). You see how impossible it is to live boxed away in a little corner of your life without interacting with other Christians. Think for a moment about the metaphor of the church as Christ's body (1 Cor. 12:12). If nothing else, it speaks to us of the interdependence of all the different parts of the body. In other words, we need each other, not least when it comes to understanding and obeying God's word. I urge you to find a church home that encourages this kind of mutual edification. If there is a pulpit ministry where you attend, make sure the teaching is sound and feedback encouraged. (A monologue need not exclude audience participation.) Make a point too of participating in small group Bible studies. Remember that believers are all on a par with each other: teachers and taught alike are fellow-sinners and fellow-learners. If possible, make room for more formal courses in the Bible. If a local church is to make a significant impact in its community it must become a learning center, a place where truth is valued and taught. (In my book *The Jesus Paradigm*, I devote an entire appendix to the theme of "Returning Biblical Education to the Local Church.")

A second thing that stands out is the importance of obedience. Knowledge itself must never be our goal. "Knowledge puffs up, but love builds up" (1 Cor. 8:1). It is not necessary for you to get a certificate in biblical studies. And please don't envy "Dr." so-and-so because of his or her degree: it is only a man-made status symbol.

At the same time, never forget that your friendship with Christ needs to be cultivated, and that loving obedience on our part is always the best response. One day a guest speaker from the Middle East ministered the word in our local fellowship. He shared with us the horrible condition of Christian slave girls in Pakistan. He concluded by telling us that it cost a mere 2,000 U.S. dollars to secure the freedom of one girl from that hideous lifestyle. Immediately I sensed the Spirit telling me to do something about it. I asked the elders for permission to speak, and then I said, "Brothers and sisters, Scripture is clear that we have an obligation to help these sisters in Christ. For does not Paul say in Romans 12:13, 'Share what you have with God's people who are in need'? Here's the first hundred dollars. Are there not 19 more of us who this very day will redeem one Pakistani girl from slavery?" Soon hands began popping up all over the room, until the need was fully met. You see, for me it was a very different thing to know what the Bible says — "Share what you have with God's people who are in need" — and then say, "So what? I don't care enough to actually do anything about it." The purpose of the Spirit's inspiring the Bible is not primarily to give us information, though He does that, but to produce in us Christlikeness of character — to make us into a people who "bear one another's burdens and so fulfill the law of Christ" (Gal. 6:5). Maybe our "financial" problems are not financial but spiritual!

A third area that strikes me is the danger of anti-intellectualism. This is the distrust of the mind. A well-known documentation of this phenomenon is Richard Hofstadter's *Anti-Intellectualism in American Life*. Christianity is a reasonable faith. I shall never forget hearing Francis Schaeffer say to a group of students in Switzerland that when people become Christians they do not have to put their brains in park or neutral. When you find the apostle Paul spending a long time in a city (say, Ephesus), it was primarily to teach. The early church worked hard on training new disciples. If the spiritual life needs nourishment, so does the intellectual. Exegetical skills are especially important in our day when people are increasingly allergic to the hard work of digging out scriptural truth for themselves. The Bible forbids us from being like animals that are "without

understanding" and commands us to be "mature" in our understanding (Psalm 32:9; 1 Cor. 14:29). "It is fundamental with us,"
wrote John Wesley, "that to renounce reason is to renounce religion,
that religion and reason go hand in hand, and that all irrational
religion is false religion" (cited in R. W. Burtner and R. E. Chiles,
A Compend of Wesley's Theology, p. 26). The plain truth is that God
created us as rational beings. Anti-intellectualism is therefore a serious threat to balanced Christianity. It is a combination of intellect
and emotion that we must always strive after.

This brings me to my final observation. Despite our commitment to apostolic teaching, there will always remain a good many
uncertainties and doubts about this or that doctrine. We will simply
have to live with these. I am a Baptist. The publisher of this book is
a Methodist. Doesn't that smack of compromise on his part? That
is an accusation that is often made, but there is no truth to it. It is
possible to be certain about what you believe without being smug.
It really comes down to this: humility. I remember attending a
conference several years ago at Trinity Evangelical Divinity School.
The conference was called "Evangelical Affirmations." Kenneth
Kanzter had assembled two professors from every major evangelical
seminary in North America. For two weeks we discussed Christian
doctrine. It immediately became clear to us that there was plenty
to disagree about. Some felt that the sign gifts were only tem-
porary. Others believed that they were still valid today. But both
sides agreed that the ministry of the Spirit was indispensable for
Christian living. Christians are meant to be in no doubt about that.

We are to be wary, of course, of false teaching. As we see from
the book of Galatians, Christians are dangerously liable to add
something to the work of Christ and His sole sufficiency. For this
reason, and many others, we should do well to be cautious of anything that deviates (or seems to deviate) from orthodox Christian
belief. But there is much that unites Christians, and we should
thank God that this is so. The best thing about Scripture is that it
draws us to the Savior who is the perfect example of how we are
to live. This change into Jesus' likeness will not happen overnight,
of course. We will still know the power of besetting sin. We will

never get over how gut-wrenching the battle with evil can be. But once we have Christ within us, the process of becoming Christlike will go on all throughout our lives, until one day all the barriers have been removed and nothing stands between us and the Lord.

Until then, let us continue to devote ourselves, both as individuals and as congregations, to the apostles' teaching!

4 GENUINE RELATIONSHIPS

"They devoted themselves to ... the fellowship."

We saw in Chapter 1 that the earliest Christians faithfully evangelized their neighbors. Their missionary work was both relentless and relational. And their success was amazing. Undoubtedly one of the main secrets of their impact was the outstanding care they gave to each other. To put it simply: they enjoyed a new way of life that attracted others to the Savior. One of the ways in which the new quality of their lives was seen was in their "fellowship." The Greek word Luke uses is *koinonia*. In the New Testament it has been translated as "fellowship," "participation," and "contribution." I think the best rendering here is "sharing." These early believers *shared life together*. They were of one heart and one soul, so much so that they eagerly shared their possessions with each other. They "had all things in common" (Acts 2:44). Their fellowship broke down all barriers.

This is another place where the modern church often misses the mark. Our lack of *koinonia*, of genuine relationships, presents a stumbling block to a great many people who are looking for authentic love in action. The earliest Christians succeeded where we fail because of their tremendous concern for one another. One cannot fail to notice how their *koinonia* expressed itself. We find in the New Testament a church that was devoted to at least three priorities.

In the first place, *here was a church devoted to mutual edification.* There are three New Testament passages that speak directly to this matter. In Heb. 10:24-25 we read: "Let us think of ways to spur one another on to acts of love and good works, not neglecting our meeting together, as some people do, but encouraging one another, especially now that the day of His return is drawing near." Suffice it to say that this passage is doing much more than condemning Christians who fail to attend church every Sunday!

Then there is 1 Cor. 14:26: "What should be done, then, brothers and sisters? When you come together, each one has a hymn, a teaching, a revelation, a tongue, or an interpretation. Let all things be done for edification."

A final passage is 1 Pet. 4:7-11: "The end of all things is near. Therefore, you must be serious and alert for the sake of your prayers. Above all, love one another earnestly, because love covers over a multitude of sins. Be hospitable to one another without complaining. As good stewards of the manifold grace of God, serve one another with whatever gift each of you has received. Whoever speaks must do so as one speaking the very words of God. Whoever serves must do so with the strength that God supplies, so that God may be glorified in all things through Jesus Christ, to whom belong glory and power forever and ever. Amen."

Is there not an important lesson in these texts? We shall have healthy churches and genuine *koinonia* to the degree that we are willing to use our gifts in service to others in the body of Christ. Yet how few churches seem to believe this. There is no authentic body life. There is no commitment to every-member ministry. There is no expectation that God can and does use every believer in the building up of the entire church family. There is no feeling that participation really matters. And yet in our churches pleas are forthcoming, heart-rending pleas for more participatory gatherings. If the plea is heard, the response is often, "But we've never done it that way before." The plea seems very radical, because the Christian church has departed so radically from the pattern of ministry established in the New Testament. Perhaps it is time to take stock and to reform. The above passages clearly show us that the main purpose of the gathering is not worship (which is to be 24/7, see Rom. 12:1-2) but mutual edification. All Christians are called to fulltime Christian ministry, not some. The earliest Christians knew nothing of a clergy-laity distinction. Every member of the church has a part to play in the service of God. As Emil Brunner puts it in his celebrated book *The Misunderstanding of the Church* (p. 50):

> One thing is supremely important; that all minister, and that nowhere is to be perceived a separation, or even merely a distinction, between those who do and those who do not minister, between the active and passive members of the body, between those who give and those who receive. There exists in the *Ecclesia* a universal duty and right of service, a universal readiness to serve, and at the same time the greatest possible differentiation of functions.

As we gather with our church families, then, let our purpose be body edification. Each Christian, without exception, has a ministry. That includes you. You ask, "Can I teach?" The answer, as we saw in chapter 3, is a resounding "Yes!" To be sure, teaching is a special function of overseers (who must be "able to teach," 1 Tim. 3:2), but it is not exclusively theirs (Col. 3:16). Paul allowed any member to take part in the ministry of the word if he or she was led to contribute (1 Cor. 14:26-29). "Can I baptize or serve the Lord's Supper?" Again, in the New Testament we are never told who should baptize or who should serve the bread and the cup. Both were lay celebrations. The concept of a special priestly cadre that alone could administer the "sacraments" (a term the New Testament never uses) will not stand the close scrutiny of Scripture and ought not to be allowed to stand in the way of congregational participation. If we are to see a return to a healthy body life, there has to be a revolution in the churches in the way we think about ministry. In a congregation that is small, it is possible to incorporate a time of sharing within the main gathering. In a larger congregation, small groups are marvelous opportunities to share interests and news and to minister to one another appropriately through the word and prayer. Building genuine relationships is possible whether you are meeting in a sanctuary or in a home. And anything that can help us to develop every-member ministry is to be encouraged.

In the second place, *here was a church that cared for one another*. It was a community where the warmth of personal fellowship was abundantly felt. Their love for each other was remarkable. They shared their possessions, their meals, their lives. They seem consistently to have worked outward from a genuine heart of love — the kind of love that only the Holy Spirit could shed abroad in their hearts (Rom. 5:8). They were in constant pray for each other. (We shall have more to say about prayer in Chapter 6). Their love for each other was so vibrant that it was infectious. Their gatherings, as we have seen, embodied the contributions of many. Kindness was commonplace. "Selling their possessions and goods, they gave to anyone as he or she had need," we are told in our passage (Acts 2:45). Unlike many a modern church, their giving was both costly and generous. These early Christians did not separate the spiritual from the temporal. They reasoned as follows: If the church does not care for the unwed mother, who will? If the church does not defend the defenseless in society, who will hear their cries? However you look at it, the early Christians *cared*.

We need to revive that attitude today. Are we hospitable, eagerly opening our homes to strangers? The early church was. Do we gladly provide for the needs of other Christians? The early church did. Do we minister to widows and orphans in their need? This was the way of the early church. We are called to be servants, and Jesus is looking for disciples who will serve Him *sacrificially*. God is no more interested in truth without love than He is interested in love without truth. How necessary are both! So let us serve one another. You can serve every day of the week, not only on Sunday or at Vacation Bible School. You can serve your co-worker, your neighbor, your family members, a stranger you meet in the street. You can do it!

In the third place, *here was a church where unity was valued*. We saw in our last chapter how this unity played out among the leadership of the church in New Testament times. There was no hierarchy, no senior pastor (other than Christ), no so-called first among equals. Their leadership was shared. How rarely is this seen in a modern church, even one that practices plural eldership. I am quite certain that nobody would object if the "senior pastor" in their church rescinded his title and receded into the group!

Unity was also seen in their decision-making. A feature of the early church that fascinates me is the way in which consensus was built. They spent time waiting upon God before making a decision. Today we need Robert's Rules of Order before we can decide on anything. Hardly anybody sits down nowadays to ask where the idea of voting came from. Part of the value of having every-member ministry is the weight it assigns to consensus-building. It seems to me that there are good reasons to reject our man-made method of decision-making. Not only does it lack a biblical foundation, but it undermines the example of the early church itself. In Acts 15 we read of a time when the early Christians made an important decision. Together the believers sought the will of God, and together they found it. There was nothing mechanical or business-like about their decision-making either. Their protocol was minimal, and the unity it produced was amazing. As James put it (Acts 15:28), "it has seemed good to the Holy Spirit and to us…." We vote, and leave an aggrieved minority. The early church waited upon the Spirit, and it produced a unified whole. Of course, the situation in Acts 15 need not necessarily be considered normative. But it is full of insight for us twenty-first century Christians. This way of making decisions could make a huge difference in the life of many a church today. Why do so many of our business meetings end up in shambles? Are we afraid of the work and prayer needed to come to a common mind? There was no such fear among the earliest Christians. We have a long way to go until we reach their sensitivity to the Spirit. He is well able to guide a congregation to a unanimous decision if everyone really looks to Him for guidance.

Their unity was seen, finally, in their commitment to the Great Commission. It was their one overmastering passion. They all shared the same priority in life. Jesus had instructed them as a matter of greatest importance to be His witnesses, to go and proclaim the Good News to every creature (Mark 16:15). And that is exactly what they did. For the Christians of New Testament days, evangelism was a first thing. It was energetically undertaken, at whatever the cost. And note: their willingness to obey their Master was a direct result of the ministry of the Holy Spirit in their midst. The Spirit was specifically given to the church in order to equip believers to be Christ's witnesses in an ever-widening circle (Acts 1:8). They did not just talk about going. They went. The church at Antioch was exemplary in this regard. The believers gladly sent out two of their most gifted teachers for the sake of the lost in other lands. Their sacrifice paid off handsomely. The Gospel was preached, men and women came to Christ, and new churches were planted.

In this chapter we have seen some of the marks of genuine community that characterized the early church. What a magnificent picture of life together! Maybe theirs was an idealism that cannot be repeated today. We may *talk* about community, but if we continue to behave like a group of individualists, no one will believe what we say. The picture that Luke gives us of the earliest church should make us stop and think.

Joseph Hellerman, author of *When the Church Was a Family*, has some interesting comments to make about the vitality of the church (p. 143). "It is time," he writes, "to inform our people that conversion to Christianity involves both our justification and our familification, that we gain a new Father when we respond to the gospel. It is time to communicate the biblical reality that personal salvation is a community-building event, and to trust God to change our lives and the lives of our churches accordingly." Our modern churches could learn a thing or two from the genuine relationships of the first Christians. Theirs is a shining example. And if we ask the secret of it, we do not have far to look: the secret lay in the presence of the Holy Spirit. His power is available to us all. And it is life-changing. Just imagine what the Spirit could do in our churches if He were allowed to have control. It could happen again.

CHRIST-CENTERED GATHERINGS

"They devoted themselves to ... the breaking of the bread."

Here we see a fifth mark of a New Testament church: "the breaking of the bread." Along with most commentators, I take this as a reference to the Lord's Supper. Clearly the observance of communion was a central act in the gathering of these early Christians. It was central because it was the one thing that Jesus had commanded His followers to do in remembrance of Him (1 Cor. 11:24). The centerpiece in our gatherings today is often either the pulpit or the altar. In the early church it was a table! And it was at this table that Jesus Himself became the conscious focus as both the host and the soon-returning celebrant.

And how often was the Supper observed? If we compare Acts 20:7 ("On the first day of the week, when we came together to break bread....") with Rev. 1:10 ("On the Lord's Day...."), it seems that it was observed every Lord's Day, that is, every Sunday. Why could it not be a regular observance for Christians today? So often our gatherings nowadays are man-centered. In Jerusalem, not so! There was a strong emphasis on the communal meal, on celebrating the exalted Jesus and the union of all believers with Him. Today it is not uncommon to find congregations combining a full meal and the Lord's Supper in a time of fellowship and joyful festivity. This practice is to be greatly commended. A weekly service like that can be very moving. There will be sharing and singing, a teaching or two from the Scriptures, much prayer and perhaps some weeping. And it will take time; it won't be accomplished in an hour! (As every family knows, fellowship around a table can be unpredictable.) But if that fellowship has Jesus at the center, the results can be profound.

In this chapter I want to think with you about why the Lord's Supper is so important. I wish to make three main points:

The Lord's Supper is important because it looks back at the cross.

The Lord's Supper is important because it symbolizes and even creates unity in the body.

The Lord's Supper is important because it causes us to eagerly anticipate Christ's return and, at the same time, to increase our evangelistic efforts.

The Lord's Supper is important because it looks back at the cross. The cross of Christ is a symbol of loss — shameful, abject, total loss. Yet Christ's death was also a new beginning. Those who have accepted Him receive not only the promise of eternal life but the possibility of walking daily with the Crucified One. A new life has begun, and He is with us through all the sorrows and sufferings of life. The cycle goes on and on — gain from loss, strength through weakness, life out of death. The table of the Lord is a unique witness to all of this. Here we see the glory of sacrificial love, the consciousness of His presence, the full-blown glory of His resurrection. Too often we think that Christianity is a feather bed that will shield us from life's hard knocks. The truth is that the Gospel involves a cross of suffering. The cross reminds us that God is no stranger to pain. The cross reminds us that God loves us through the pain. The cross reminds us how God uses pain to accomplish His purposes. And the cross reminds us that God ultimately triumphs over pain through the resurrection. It is here, at the cross, that the problem of pain is handled biblically. Sometimes God uses pain to instill within us such qualities as perseverance and self-sacrifice. At other times he uses pain to equip us to comfort others with the comfort by which God has comforted us. On the cross, Jesus drained the cup of suffering and emerged victorious. So can we!

The table of the Lord is also a reminder that our Creator is also our Redeemer. Christ has quenched God's wrath toward us by washing away our sins. Our Savior received the wages of sin in our place. Some gatherings of Christians are open to blame because they never get down to this level. The focus is not on Christ but on societal reformation. You ask, "Does not the Gospel offer solutions to society's problems?" Indeed it does. But the Gospel solves a much deeper problem — the fact that you and I are alienated from our Maker. Until we make the reconciling work of the Gospel plain, until we focus on the solution to the problem of mankind's relationship to God, we misrepresent the Gospel. The Gospel, then, is primarily and fundamentally the means of a new relationship with God — and the Lord's Supper is a distinct reminder of this priority.

The Lord's Supper is important because it symbolizes and even creates unity in the body. We saw in the last chapter how important unity was to these early believers. They were unified in their leadership, in their decision-making, and in their passion for evangelism. We should not, then, be surprised to see the same emphasis in the way they observed the Lord's Supper. A key passage is 1 Cor. 10:16-17:

> *The cup of blessing that we bless, is it not a sharing in the blood of Christ? The loaf of bread that we break, is it not a sharing in the body of Christ? Because there is one loaf, we who are many are one body, for we all partake of the one loaf.*

Notice what Paul does not say here. He does not say that we partake of one loaf of bread because we are one body. On the contrary! It is because we partake of the one loaf of bread that we are one body. This is an amazing truth. When someone takes from the single loaf, he or she is creating unity with the rest of the participants. This explains why Paul is so insistent that there be only one loaf. It is also the reason why he commands the believers in Corinth to wait until all are present before participating. When a local assembly of Christians gathers to partake of the bread and the cup, the members are made one body by virtue of their common participation in the Lord's Supper. The context suggests that Paul was thinking of the Corinthians' disunity and factionalism. How easy it is for the rich to eat before the poor arrive! In ways like this, says Paul, we grieve the Holy Spirit and rob ourselves of His powerful and gracious work in our midst.

I sense reluctance in many parts of the church today to accept this instruction from Paul. His language seems to require singularity of the bread and, by extension, of the cup. Other forms of communion (broken crackers and tiny cups), while perhaps more practical, fail to give significance to the importance Paul attached to the oneness aspect of the Supper. It is the work of the Holy Spirit to unite Christ's body, not to divide it. At all times and in all places we are responsible to "preserve the unity of the Spirit in the bond of peace" (Eph. 4:3). And that means being open to the Spirit's teaching through the apostle here in 1 Cor. 10:16-17. The idea of a single loaf of bread may be a most unfashionable doctrine today, but it is unquestionably the teaching of the New Testament.

The Lord's Supper is important because it causes us to eagerly anticipate Christ's return and, at the same time, to increase our evangelistic efforts. As Christians, we shall want to contest the assumption of most of our contemporaries in the West that this life is all there is. Our earthly existence is merely a foretaste of eternity. We dare not, therefore, be bound by a focus on the here-and-now. Eternity looms; Jesus is coming again! It is the kingdom of heaven we seek, not the kingdom of men. Is this not a focus of the Lord's Supper? For it is here, at the table of the Lord, that we are reminded again and again of Jesus' return. "Every time you eat this bread and drink from this cup you proclaim the Lord's death until He comes" (1 Cor. 11:26). And what a coming that will be! Christ's first coming was marked by great humiliation. His second coming will be in great majesty. He will come, not as Savior, but as Judge, and He will usher in the kingdom that was inaugurated when He first entered the world. The Christian must not forget this forward-looking aspect of Christianity. The earliest believers knew that "The Lord is at hand!" (Phil. 4:5). So thank Him that He is alive, that He knows you and loves you, that He is at work in your life, and that He is coming again to right all wrongs. That is something to rejoice about!

Of course, a future-focus is no excuse for passivity in the present. It is tragic when Christians fail to see that the doctrine of Christ's second coming is more than a matter for theological discussion and debate. Ought not His imminent return prompt us to greater obedience? Ought not His second coming create in us a greater sense of urgency to share the Gospel with those around us who are lost? Ought not the return of the King spur us on to greater involvement in Calvary-like acts of service in the world? There is no higher priority for the church than to heed the Savior's command to make disciples of all nations. "The Lord is at hand!" Now is the time to re-examine our consciences, reevaluate our priorities, reappropriate the forgiveness Christ won for us on the cross, and rededicate our lives to taking the Good News to the ends of the earth.

The Lord's Supper, then, must never be allowed to turn inward on itself. We are to proclaim the Lord's death until He comes. It simply will not do to memorialize Christ's death. There has got to be the outworking of the Lord's Supper in our daily lives. Otherwise we shall find dullness and apathy in our gatherings. Genuine anticipation of Christ's return and genuine work on His behalf in the world go hand in hand. They cannot be separated if either is to remain healthy. Even as we are to pray "Come, Lord Jesus!" (Rev. 22:20), so we are to pray "Your kingdom come, Your will be done, on earth as it is in heaven" (Matt. 6:10). Pray for the extension of God's kingdom in the hearts of those in your circle (and beyond) who do not give Him their allegiance. Seek to do all you can to extend His kingly rule in society. Practice walking in daily communion with your risen and soon-returning Lord. Christ is your Friend, and you can turn to Him at any moment of the day. In a word, live as though He were coming back today — not by sitting around idly staring into heaven but, like Jesus before you, doing all you can to "seek and to save that which was lost" (Luke 19:10). There is no joy like it.

FERVENT PRAYER

"They devoted themselves ... to the prayers."

Do you believe in prayer? The early church did. There are few things stressed more in the book of Acts than the reality of God's work in answering the prayers of His people. Our text puts it this way: "They devoted themselves ... to the prayers." What does the plural "prayers" imply? At the very least, it suggests that these believers prayed often and even had stated times of corporate prayer. Does that characterize your church? Mine?

Recently I had a long conversation with an Ethiopian about prayer. He was frankly shocked at the prayerlessness of American churches. There are hundreds of church-planned activities but few prayer meetings. Even our Wednesday-night "prayer services" are little more than Bible studies with a few minutes of "bless-me" prayers attached. How can we ever hope to reach a lost world unless we are a people of prayer?

In the book of Acts, we find Christians prioritizing prayer. Prior to Pentecost we find the apostles devoting themselves to prayer, along with Mary the mother of Jesus and His brothers (1:14). The church prayed when they appointed the seven servants to assist the neglected widows (6:6). When the Holy Spirit chose Barnabas and Saul to evangelize the lost, it was a church at prayer that sent them out (13:3). Paul prayed when he appointed leaders in every congregation (14:23). When faced with persecution, the church prayed (4:23-31). Peter and John prayed for the Samaritans (8:15), while Paul and Silas prayed in prison (16:25). Paul prayed with the Ephesian elders (20:36), with the believers near Tyre (21:5), in the Jerusalem temple (22:17), in the presence of the 276 persons aboard ship (27:35), and for the father of Publius at Malta (28:8). If, then, we ask what role prayer played in the life of the early church, the answer is plain enough. The church was birthed and lived in an atmosphere of prayer.

During my seventeen visits to Ethiopia in the past ten years, I have witnessed a similar level of commitment. Day-long prayer meetings are not uncommon. Church leaders spend time together in prayer daily. With few exceptions, every local church has prayer teams that meet at least once a week for a time of intensive prayer. These believers did not always pray this way. Their prayer life was molded in the crucible of years of persecution and suffering. It will require, perhaps, no less of a testing if the New Testament pattern of prayer is to be realized among us. It is nothing for Ethiopian Christians to set aside entire days for fasting and prayer. Why aren't we doing the same? You will seldom find churches with prayer services any more, let alone all-day prayer meetings. It seems that we can't wait for God. We have transferred our faith from God to modern business management models. God is eager to give us good things, things that we desperately need, but He expects us to ask for those things, and to ask expectantly. All Christians are called to a life of prayer. The New Testament church was born in a prayer meeting (Acts 1:14), and Paul's writings are filled with so many injunctions to pray that it almost seems as though he spent his entire ministry enjoying a well-practiced intimacy with God.

But what is prayer? And how is it possible?

There are many ways of defining prayer, but perhaps the foundational notion is that of communing with God. Prayer is an attitude as well as activity; it is both communion and communication. One of the most significant ways of defining biblical prayer is by examining the Greek words used to describe it in the New Testament. Of these the word *proseuche* is far and away the most significant. Along with its verbal form *proseuchomai*, it is used well over 100 times in the New Testament, 25 times in the book of Acts alone. *Proseuche* involves speaking to God, but it goes much further than that. It is as much a Godward attitude on the part of the Christian as it is an act. We might call it an *attitude of prayerfulness*. Thus Paul can command Christians to "pray without ceasing" (1 Thess. 5:17). Here the thought is not one of a continuous conversation with the Almighty. At this moment, I am typing this book, not praying. Am I therefore disobeying this command? You see, the type of praying that Paul is referring to is not so much the uttering of words to God as it is enjoying fellowship with Him. We might say that prayer is ultimately communing with our Lord. I think of the Keswick Movement's emphasis on "practicing the presence" of Christ. Prayer begins with a conscious awareness of the Savior's presence. Little or nothing will be accomplished in our prayer life without this personal relationship. Prayer is just friends being together. Sometimes words are involved, and sometimes they are not. Do you know people who enjoy a deep relationship with the Lover of their souls? There you will find prayerful people.

But there is much more that can and must be said about the nature of prayer. Three other Greek words require our attention. First we have *deesis*. A *deesis* is a petition. Then we have *aitema*. An *aitema* is the basic New Testament word for "request." Finally, we have *eucharistia*. This word refers to the giving of thanks. These words refer, not to different kinds of prayer, but to different aspects of prayer. Putting them all together, we might say that prayer is communing with God our Father, to whom we come with our petitions and requests, and whom we praise and thank for His goodness and faithfulness to us. If a church is to be healthy, it will not happen without this kind of praying. But how is prayer even possible?

The answer is: It is not. Nothing describes the Christian's weakness and inability like his or her prayer life. Rom. 8:26-27 is highly instructive at this point. Here Paul conceives of prayer as the ministry of the Holy Spirit within us. Implied is the complete inability of the Christian to pray without divine assistance and participation. In a sense, Paul is saying that prayer is ultimately an inter-Trinitarian process: God speaking to God through us. This is a profound truth and a remarkable paradox. I cannot pray unless the Holy Spirit prays; but the Holy Spirit will not pray unless I am praying! Perhaps this is what Paul is alluding to when in Eph. 6:18 he says that Christians are to be "praying at all times in the Spirit." Some exegetes regard this as a reference to praying "in tongues."

But there seems to be little reason to hold this view. Praying in tongues may well be included, but Paul's language is broad enough to include any kind of prayer we might offer. Paul's main point is that prayer must cease to be a do-it-yourself activity. It is the Spirit, and the Spirit alone, who activates, empowers, and enables prayer. There is a fine sense of realism in all this. Do not think for a moment that you can pray without the Spirit's help. Be sensitive to His promptings. When He leads you to pray, pray! There is no alternative means of prayer. The Spirit is *the* enabler of prayer.

Each of us, in our own daily walk with God, is confronted with trials and stressors. These test our faith and should cause us to spend more time communing with God in prayer. If we did this, the result would be a deeper dependence on God. How can we overcome the unseen spiritual forces arrayed against us unless we are a people of prayer? God's people always move forward on their knees. Tell God everything that is in your heart. Speak to Him as you would to a dear friend. And be sure to offer your prayers "in the name of Christ," as Jesus Himself instructed us (John 14:13-14; 16:23-28). Praying in Jesus' name is not some kind of magical password that can be used indiscriminately to get our way. Prayer in Jesus' name is effective only when we are praying in a manner that is both consistent with our relationship to Christ and God's will. Prayer involves adjusting and even relinquishing our expectations and plans to the will of the Father.

In his book *The Practice of the Presence of God*, Brother Lawrence writes that some of his closest moments with God were not spent on his knees but by staying in constant communion with Him throughout the day. Try "practicing the presence" yourself in the midst of the noise and confusion of your day. Remember that you can pray in the shower, while jogging, or even while sitting in class bored to death. Whenever the Spirit brings the words of prayer to mind, immediately respond, whether that response is a desperate "Help!" or a quick "Thanks!" Prayer is nothing more than voicing our dependence upon the true and living God. And the answer to each and every prayer that we offer is the same: He is with us, making up for all of our weakness with all of His power.

7 SACRIFICIAL LIVING

"All the believers continued together in close fellowship and shared everything they had with one another. They would sell their property and possessions and distribute the money among all, according to what each person needed."

The final mark of a New Testament church is sacrificial living. If God's overall plan in sending His Son is to equip His church for mission, we may well ask what that mission looks like. The Spirit's activity in the church, in terms of evangelism and fellowship, must be balanced by driving its members out into a needy world. Examine Acts 2:43-47 and you will notice that salvation of necessity leads to service. It cannot be otherwise. The Spirit who was sent at Pentecost is supremely the Servant of the Lord. You can go no higher in the Christian life than when you stoop to wash the feet of others. Until there is a genuine spirit of giving, until there is a real sharing of money and possessions, a lost world is unlikely to remark about the quality of our fellowship. There has been a disastrous tendency for some Christians to so emphasize "soul-winning" at the expense of the "social gospel" that their message falls on deaf ears. The idea of separating the spiritual from the social never occurred to the earliest Christians. Their love for each other was truly amazing. Without it there could be no effective evangelism. Without it the world would remain unimpressed by the Gospel. No, instead of retreating into their cloistered monasteries, instead of separating the spiritual from the social, these early Christians made the out-working of the love of God in a fallen world a priority. Not to put too fine an edge on it, they were a people guilty of scandalous love.

As I think of how those who came to faith in Christ through the preaching of Peter proclaimed the Gospel by living it, I believe the greatest single ingredient in their success was their love for Christ. Followers of Jesus gradually became like Him. The result was a church that truly cared for the poor and needy. Non-Christians were intrigued by this change and wanted to know its cause.

So today, the world is looking for genuine relationships, and until it sees love in action it will not be very interested in what Christians have to say. I remember discussing this during my first trip to Ethiopia in 2004. My wife and I had encountered a young blind boy who was selling trinkets in a secluded village. We thought nothing of it until we had returned to the States. One day my wife asked me, "Honey, do you remember that blind boy in Ethiopia? Do you think there is something we can do for him?" We prayed about it, and the Lord led us to provide a cornea transplant for that little boy. During his recovery in the capital city of Addis Ababa, we arranged for him to stay at a Mennonite college where I had previously taught Greek. There, he came to faith in Christ. He asked a student, "Why does everybody love me so much? And why do Dr. and Mrs. Black love me so much?" That student shared with him the love of Christ, and that day this young boy became my brother in Christ. I have since had the privilege of sharing the Gospel with many Muslims in Ethiopia, not a few of whom have come to believe in Christ. "Why," they would ask, "would you leave America and come here to my village and live in my hut with me and eat my food?" And I would tell them about One who left all the glory of heaven to come to this earth to die on a stinking, filthy, bloody Roman cross for the sins of the world.

The Gospel and social concern go hand in hand. Both are essential to the Great Commission. Individual conversion should always lead to social responsibility. It is a scandal when Christians separate their Christian faith from social involvement. In short, God is in the business of saving individuals who in turn will share the responsibility for evangelism and social action. This is exactly what the church in Acts 2 did. Here we see no false compartmentalization of faith. Evangelism led, and led immediately, to social action. Of course, within the process, evangelism took the front seat. Evangelism was the beginning of a social conscience. All genuine social action is but the outgrowth of personal salvation.

Christians today need to recover this thoroughly Gospel-based focus. Only a genuine commitment to the Great Commission can withstand the acids of easy-believism on the one hand and misguided humanitarianism on the other. The "evangelism mandate" must lead to the "cultural mandate." We cannot insist on the priority of personal conversion without a recognition that genuine conversion implies a fundamental social responsibility. All too often Christians concentrate on proclaiming the Gospel without living the Gospel. In reaction, others emphasize social action to the point where the message of salvation gets lost amidst the noise of building hospitals, school buildings, and wells. And the earliest Christians? The idea of separating spiritual conversion from practical deeds of love never occurred to them. They both proclaimed and lived the Gospel. These early Christians had a genuine concern for those around them. So intense was their concern that they became famous for their deep, loving, practical assistance in times of need. The church of Acts was outward-looking. Suffice it to say that "fellowship" for them meant more than a potluck supper. Here was a church that gave generously to support their own, even across barriers of race and nationality (see Acts 6). What a splendid example for the church of today!

My experience as a global missionary goes to support the claim that once the love of Christ grabs hold of you, you will never be content with living "the good Christian life" any longer. I have taken countless teams with me to Ethiopia — people who were willing to travel across cultures to encourage their brothers and sisters. In this way we glimpsed something of the catholicity of the body of Christ. We are all part of the one church of God. We support each other. We pray for each other. When necessary, we assist each other financially. And the result? Both home and overseas churches are enriched and edified.

There are some church members who have the ability to teach practical skills overseas. I recall taking a farmer with me one year to southern Ethiopia to teach the farmers there about bloat in cattle.

He gave agricultural workshops and distributed high-protein seeds to the farmers he met. On top of all this, he shared with them the love of Christ and lived Christ's love before their very eyes. I know many others — doctors, nurses, schoolteachers — who have had similar ministries on other teams we've taken with us to Africa. Like the early Christians, they realized that the Gospel must be preached to the lost, and like the early Christians, they refused to drive a wedge between the personal Gospel and the social gospel. How we need that balance today!

I have always found it fascinating that the same Greek word (*koinonia*) can be translated "fellowship" and "financial contribution." The earliest Christians were *giving* Christians. They were a family, and so they took care of each other. Their love so impressed the world that people exclaimed, "See how these Christians love one another!" Now do you see why Jesus said, "It is hard for someone who is rich to enter the kingdom of heaven!" (Matt. 19:23). He who told others to give themselves away for the poor did that very thing himself. As Paul puts it, "For you know the grace of our Lord Jesus Christ. Though He was rich, for your sake He became poor, so that you through His poverty might become rich" (2 Cor. 8:9). And we are to follow in His steps. Christianity broke the back of greed. "The power of the life-giving spirit of Christ has set me free from the power of sin and death" (Rom. 8:2)

That pretty much sums up Christian ethics. Christians are not enslaved to a set of man-made rules. Christ has set us free. The focus of behavior is therefore no longer external. It is internal, as the Holy Spirit enables us to live as Christ lived — sacrificially and even scandalously. Thank goodness that many today are willing to let God touch their wallets. I think of a grandmother who gave $100 dollars for Ethiopia in lieu of giving her grandchildren Christmas presents they didn't even need. I think of an American woman who spent three months in Ethiopia caring for a pregnant woman at great personal cost. How is it done? Christians who have experienced love give love. Rather than hoarding their wealth, they have learned the habit of using their resources deliberately and joyfully for others.

Sacrificial living, then, is tremendously important for the Christian. This does not mean that Christians will never spend anything on themselves. There needs to be a balance to our use of money. Paul is clear that we are to make provisions for our families (1 Tim. 5:8). But does this not also include our spiritual family? Will it not involve giving to missions? Should we not leave at least a portion of our estate to Christian work? There are plenty of needs to go around. The Lord will show you where you can be of greatest usefulness, if you are open to His leading.

As we saw in Chapter 4, the church is not a mere humanitarian organization. It is a community that transcends all barriers. I love it when Luke writes in our passage, "All the believers continued together in close fellowship and shared everything they had with one another." It is difficult to overestimate the power of love. This is God's strategy for societal change. He creates a fellowship of men and women who have been set free from the charms of material- ism. Can we humble ourselves and learn from these first century Christians? To be sure, our setting is far different from theirs. But we can learn many invaluable principles to try here in the West. In much of our Western Christianity we have lost the joy of sacrificial giving. "We tithe to ourselves," is how one pastor put it to me. We have lost the sense of global community. Is it too much to hope that a similar manifestation of generosity might be seen in our churches in this country?

I do not question the fact that salvation is personal and indi- vidual, but it is far more than that. However, for many evangelicals the emphasis on the personal and individual has increasingly made salvation individualistic. The whole of the Christian experience is thought to be one's personal relationship to God — often to the exclusion of one's relationship with others or to the culture in general. I prefer a more balanced approach. Since sin is personal, each individual is guilty of sin and must be forgiven for his or her sin, not someone else's. However, salvation is also social. Jesus is Lord of all. Politics, education, economics, the arts — all these are included under His divine Lordship. Thus Christians must come to understand that although salvation is individual and personal, the kingdom of God is far broader than just our personal salvation experiences.

For example, I can say (and I say it with regret) that I have led people to Christ without any follow up whatsoever. That is, I failed to emphasize the Lordship demands of Christ in a way that would have encouraged them to get involved in a local body of believers where they could be taught to observe what Jesus commanded them, including His love command (John 13:35). In the preface to his 1739 *Hymn Book*, John Wesley wrote, "The Gospel of Christ knows no religion but social, no holiness but social holiness." Therefore we must face the question: for the one who has a personal relationship with Jesus Christ, is it really possible to serve Him without displaying a genuine love and concern for others?

As player-coaches, elders must encourage their flocks to be all that God is calling them to be in the world — people who are truthful, loving, and caring, trying to change conditions that are not in harmony with God's will, and seeking to meet the needs of others — physically, emotionally, spiritually, economically, educationally. We need to "play the music" before non-believers will "hear the words." We must do everything possible, through love and good deeds, to show them the love and goodness of God and help them to see that proper human relationships are possible only through a proper relationship with Christ. Indeed, it is Christ's love that frees us from our sins to truly love others (John 8:36-38; Gal. 5:13).

This is not a new program to promote. This is just living out our Christianity — cleaning out shut-ins' gutters, raking their leaves, sawing their fallen limbs after an ice storm, having an "open door" policy at our homes and offices, gently but firmly defending the faith in our homes and in the public square, loving our unsaved neighbors enough to confront them with their lostness, etc. With joy we are to go all out with both emphases — to love God with our whole hearts, and to love our neighbors as ourselves.

Paul once referred to Christian fellowship as "the perfect bond of love" (Col. 3:14), for only love has the adhesive power to hold the whole body together. True orthodoxy kills self-centeredness; it puts an end to our private desires and ambitions. It makes a person less willing to argue a point of theology as long as there are lost people to be saved and spiritually sick Christians to be healed. In the light of the cross we discover that sharing the love of Jesus with others, whether in the far-distant villages of Ethiopia or in the sun-drenched farms of southern Virginia, is true wealth and satisfaction. You cannot at one and the same time believe in the Gospel of Jesus Christ and the gospel of self-fulfillment. There is but one possible escape from our dead orthodoxy and our smug fundamentalism, and that is for us to assess everything assiduously in the light of the love that loved us and gave itself for us.

There is, I fear, a kind of Christianity that delights in being harsh and almost brutal. Strength is present, and so is doctrinal purity, but there is no tact or compassion. No one ever lived a holier life than Jesus, yet our Great High Priest is full of sympathy, mercy, and grace. He bears with us without getting irritated or annoyed. His very patience and understanding woo us back to the right path. With Christ we are always safe. The lesson? It is at least threefold. To remember that words are cheap but deeds are costly. To remember that the thousands (or perhaps millions) of words that I have uttered in speeches or published in books are useless — in fact less than useless, a positive impediment — if they are not backed up by simple deeds of courtesy. And finally, to remember that the purpose of the inspired Scripture is always a supremely practical one — that the servant of God may be fully equipped for every good work (2 Tim. 3:16-17). In his book *Enigma of the Cross* (p. 174), Alister McGrath says it more eloquently than I ever could:

> Mission and theology are so clearly interrelated that they cannot be permitted to become divorced in the manner which western academic theologians have become accustomed. After all, in Jesus Christ God himself came down to earth, down to the level of us mortals, and it ought not to be beyond the capacities of theologians to do the same. Theology must come down to earth, to serve the church and its mission in the world — and if it will not come down to earth, it must be *brought* down to earth by

so marginalising academic theology within the life of the church that it ceases to have relevance to that church, in order that a theological orientation towards the pastoral and missiological needs of the church may develop in its wake.

It is, then, no longer possible (if it ever was) to assume that theology can operate apart from service to the world. The more we understand the Scriptures, the more we understand our responsibility to submit our lives and our futures to its radical teachings. Once this is recognized, then social compassion will truly be an apostolic focus of the church's apostolic function. Instead of doing theology for theology's sake, we will choose to bear witness to the Gospel in both word and deed, by both lip and life. We will, perhaps, also do less pontificating from our ivory towers high up in cyberspace and descend to the balcony, and maybe even to the ground floor.

Should that, by the grace of God, ever happen, the nations would witness theology come down to earth, where it truly belongs.

The Jesus Paradigm

David Alan Black

Black writes an immensely practical book that will rearrange the furniture in your mind and, if heeded, will resurrect biblical Christianity.

David B. Capes
Professor in Christianity, Houston Baptist University

I for one couldn't put it down, and I read it in one sitting.

Craig Bennett
Trinitarian Dance

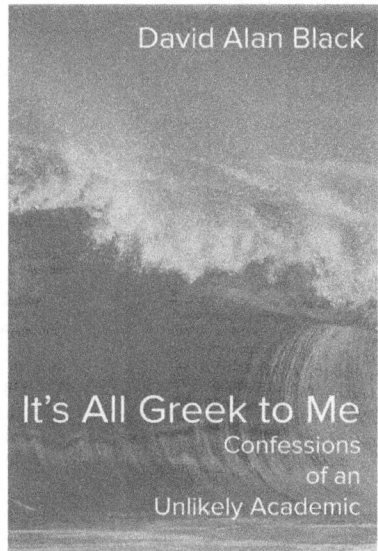

David Alan Black

It's All Greek to Me
Confessions of an Unlikely Academic

More from Energion Publications

Personal Study

Holy Smoke! Unholy Fire	Bob McKibben	$14.99
The Jesus Paradigm	David Alan Black	$17.99
When People Speak for God	Henry Neufeld	$17.99
The Sacred Journey	Chris Surber	$11.99

Christian Living

It's All Greek to Me	David Alan Black	$3.99
Grief: Finding the Candle of Light	Jody Neufeld	$8.99
My Life Story	Becky Lynn Black	$14.99
Crossing the Street	Robert LaRochelle	$16.99
Life as Pilgrimage	David Moffett-Moore	14.99

Bible Study

Learning and Living Scripture	Lentz/Neufeld	$12.99
From Inspiration to Understanding	Edward W. H. Vick	$24.99
Philippians: A Participatory Study Guide	Bruce Epperly	$9.99
Ephesians: A Participatory Study Guide	Robert D. Cornwall	$9.99
Ecclesiastes: A Participatory Study Guide	Russell Meek	$9.99

Theology

Creation in Scripture	Herold Weiss	$12.99
Creation: the Christian Doctrine	Edward W. H. Vick	$12.99
The Politics of Witness	Allan R. Bevere	$9.99
Ultimate Allegiance	Robert D. Cornwall	$9.99
History and Christian Faith	Edward W. H. Vick	$9.99
The Journey to the Undiscovered Country	William Powell Tuck	$9.99
Process Theology	Bruce G. Epperly	$4.99

Ministry

Clergy Table Talk	Kent Ira Groff	$9.99
Out of This World	Darren McClellan	$24.99

Generous Quantity Discounts Available
Dealer Inquiries Welcome
Energion Publications — P.O. Box 841
Gonzalez, FL_ 32560
Website: http://energionpubs.com
Phone: (850) 525-3916

www.ingramcontent.com/pod-product-compliance
Lightning Source LLC
Chambersburg PA
CBHW031613040426
42452CB00006B/508